LEARN
TOGETHER

TEST YOUR REASONING 2

Words, diagrams and shapes

Roy Childs

Illustrated by Graham Butler

MACMILLAN
CHILDREN'S BOOKS

Just for Fun!

Suggestions for activities to help your reasoning skills

In everyday life we are always solving problems. Deciding which is the best bike to buy or the quickest way to get to a friend's house involves reasoning and problem solving. Some of us are better than others at certain kinds of reasoning but usually not at all kinds of reasoning. The tests in this booklet might show that you find words easier to deal with than diagrams, for example. If you want to try to improve your reasoning skills you have to practise them. It is probably true that solving any kind of problem helps you to develop your general reasoning, but some activities are better than others for developing certain kinds of reasoning. Below are some suggestions for activities which involve solving problems which might help to improve your reasoning skills.

1. Verbal Reasoning Skills

Any games that make you more familiar with words are useful. Crosswords, hangman or scrabble are all good examples. Try to play more games which concentrate on words. Traditional English exercises as done in school help a lot, too.

2. Non-Verbal Reasoning Skills

Games involving logic, sequences, and classification can all be useful. Card games, more and more difficult jigsaw puzzles, books of puzzles, chess, draughts, and Kim's game all require you to reason in ways other than just with words.

3. Spatial Reasoning Skills

Playing games like 'I spy' can help you notice differences and similarities in the world around you. Noticing how they change when looked at from different angles, or playing with shapes, cubes, Lego, or playing 'GO', or card games such as 'pairs' all may help you develop better spatial reasoning skills.

The above suggestions may help you to improve your reasoning skills in the different areas tested by this booklet but, just as valuable, is practice in all the subjects and skills you learn at school. Think about some of these, too, and practise them when you can.

First published in the Practise Together series 1987
by Pan Books Ltd

Published 1992 as *Test Your Reasoning*
by Pan Macmillan Children's Books

This edition published 1996 by Macmillan Children's Books
a division of Macmillan Publishers Limited
25 Eccleston Place, London SW1W 9NF
and Basingstoke

Associated companies throughout the world

ISBN 0 330 32654 6

Text copyright © Roy Childs 1987
Illustrations copyright © Graham Butler 1987

The moral right of the author has been asserted.

9 8 7

Photoset by Parker Typesetting Service, Leicester
Printed and bound in India by Gopsons Papers Ltd,
Noida 201 301

Before you start

This book is designed for your child to test his or her reasoning ability at home. A detailed introduction is given in the tinted pull-out section between pages 14 and 15. The answer key is also in this section. In case you want your child to work through the tests without access to the answers, you can pull out the tinted section carefully and keep it separately. (You may have to push back the staples slightly.)

So, before your child starts work, turn to the middle and read the suggestions on how to use the book.

Unit One

Look at these words:

Long → Short   Big → Small

You can see that Long and Short go together because they are opposites. Big and Small are also opposites. In this test the question will look like this.

	A	B	C	D
Long → Short as Big →	Tall	Wide	(C) Small	Narrow

You can see that choice C – Small has been circled to show that Small goes with Big in the same way as the two words Long and Short.
Now try this example and put a ring round your choice before reading on.

	A	B	C	D
Curtain → Window as Carpet →	Wool	Floor	Lino	Red

You should have chosen B – Floor. A curtain covers a window and so a carpet covers the floor. If you are not sure what to do ask someone now. Otherwise begin the test.

Test One starts here

		A	B	C	D
1.	Bracelet → Arm as Ring →	Finger	Foot	Hoop	Circle
2.	Spade → Dig as Knife →	Eat	Cut	Metal	Edge
3.	Cap → Head as Shoe →	Toe	Foot	Hair	Walk
4.	Tongue → Taste as Eye →	Sight	Smell	Light	Dark
5.	Slow → Fast as Low →	Short	High	Tall	Tide

4

		A	B	C	D
6.	Free → Expensive as Silence →	Quiet	Noise	Golden	Rich

		A	B	C	D
7.	Stream → River as Sea →	Pond	Ocean	Wet	Salt

		A	B	C	D
8.	Noise → Tune as Smell →	Dog	Waft	Scent	Nose

		A	B	C	D
9.	Brick → House as Page →	Cover	Number	Leaf	Book

		A	B	C	D
10.	Fish → Water as Bird →	Feather	Air	Wind	Wings

		A	B	C	D
11.	Blind → Eye as Deaf →	Lobe	Ear	Shout	Hear

		A	B	C	D
12.	Branch → Stick as Trunk →	Dead	Apple	Rod	Log

		A	B	C	D
13.	Metre → Distance as Hour →	Second	Time	Unit	Watch

		A	B	C	D
14.	Want → Desire as Need →	Require	Wish	Request	Use

		A	B	C	D
15.	Apple → Pear as Potato →	Eat	Chip	Plum	Turnip

			A	B	C	D
16.	Big → Large	as Small →	Little	Low	Short	Tall
17.	Wheel → Circular	as Tube →	Pipe	Oil	Square	Cylindrical
18.	Water → Drink	as Fruit →	Tree	Plum	Eat	Dish
19.	Birth → Death	as Begin →	Live	Start	Race	End
20.	Past → Future	as Gone →	Went	Bone	Coming	Had
21.	Hair → Barber	as Nail →	Claw	Scratch	Hand	Manicurist
22.	Walk→Locomotion	as Talk →	Shout	Mouth	Voice	Communication
23.	Foot → Paw	as Nail →	Hand	Long	Claw	Metal
24.	Hill → Valley	as Plateau →	Beach	Plain	Mountain	Flat
25.	Hole → Trench	as Bucket →	Pail	White	Trough	Leak

Unit One   1–25
Score

6

Unit Two

In this test you will be given some information written inside a box. This information is always correct. You will be asked to decide which of the four statements below it must also be correct. Look at this example:

> Tom is older than Mary.   Mary is older than Ali.

always correct

A	B	C	D
Ali is older than Mary.	Ali is older than Tom.	Tom is the oldest.	Mary is the oldest.

Choice (A) cannot be correct because the box tells us that Mary is older than Ali. Now read the other choices and decide which is correct before reading on.

The answer is (C). All the others are wrong. To show this we have put a circle around (C) to show it is the only correct answer. Now try this example.

> Whales are very big.   This elephant is very big.

A	B	C	D
This elephant is a whale.	Elephants are whales.	All grown elephants are big.	Whales and elephants. can be big.

You may have wanted to choose C. You know that grown elephants are big. This test does not ask 'what do *you* know?' but asks 'what does the information in the box tell you?' Here it tells you that 'this elephant is very big'. The box does not tell you that this is true of all elephants but it does tell us that it can be true. So D is the correct answer.

If you are unsure ask someone to explain before you do the test. When you are happy that you understand, begin the test on page 8.

Test Two starts here

1. | Terry is younger than Anne.   Satpel is younger than Terry.

A
Terry is the youngest.

B
Satpel is the youngest.

C
Terry is younger than Satpel.

D
Anne is younger than Satpel.

2. | Richard has 4 sweets.   Raj and Stephen have 3 sweets each.

A
Raj has the most sweets.

B
Stephen has the most sweets.

C
Richard has the the least number of sweets.

D
Richard, Raj and Stephen together have 10 sweets.

3. | Peter is very tall.   Paul is taller than Peter.

A
Paul is short.

B
Paul is shorter than Peter.

C
Paul is very tall.

D
Peter is short.

4. | Mr Brown's shop has the cheapest oranges in town.   In the same town Mr West's shop sells oranges at 10p each.

A
Mr Brown's oranges cost 9p.

B
Mr Brown's oranges cost less than 10p each.

C
Mr West's oranges are very expensive.

D
Mr West's oranges are nearly as cheap as Mr Brown's.

5. | Some dogs have long tails.   All dogs have fur.

A
All dogs have fur and long tails.

B
All dogs have tails.

C
Some dogs have no fur.

D
Some dogs have long tails and fur.

6. Fred and Fran like playing football. Fred and Andrew like watching football. Andrew and Fran like playing basketball.

A	B	C	D
Fran likes playing both games.	Fran likes watching football.	Andrew likes watching both games.	Andrew likes playing both games.

7. Tim plays tennis. Some tennis players are good badminton players.

A	B	C	D
Tim is not a good badminton player.	Tim is a good badminton player.	Tim doesn't like badminton.	Tim might be a good badminton player.

8. Apples grow on trees. Pears and apples are both fruit.

A	B	C	D
All fruit grows on trees.	Some fruit grows on trees.	Pears must grow on trees.	Pears must grow on bushes.

9. All motor cars have wheels. All motor cars need fuel.

A	B	C	D
Whatever has wheels and needs fuel is a motor car.	Some things which have wheels and need fuel are motor cars.	All things which have wheels are motor cars.	All things which need fuel have wheels.

10. If a tennis racket has no strings it is useless. Some tennis rackets are useless.

A	B	C	D
All useful tennis rackets have strings.	Some tennis rackets have no strings.	Some useful tennis rackets have no strings.	All tennis rackets with strings are useful.

Unit Two 1–10
Score

Unit Three

1. Underline the 2 words which must change places.

   The lake swam in the boy

2. Fill in the missing number.

   3, 6, 9, (_____), 15, 18

3. If ADDQ means BEER what does FHQK means? (_____)

4. Underline the two words, one from each set of brackets, which have almost opposite meanings.

   (seat, sit, chair)   (walk, run, stand)

5. Write in a letter which will end the first and begin the second word.

   WEE(.....)ROWL

6. What is the next letter?

   A B A D A F A (___)

7. Underline the word that should go in the middle if they were arranged in order.

   walk   stand   sprint   run   jog

8. Underline the two words which must change places.

   It was an afternoon eventful after all

9. Write down the next in this series.

   AZ, BY, CX, DW, (_____)

10. Underline the word in brackets which can go with both pairs of words at each end of the bracket.

    autumn, summer (winter, spring, bounce, run) jump, leap

11. If 42974 means TIGHT, what does 724 mean? (_____)

12. Underline the two words, one from each set of brackets, which mean most nearly the same.

    (hint, tint, flint)   (flu, true, clue)

13. Write in a letter which will end the first and begin the second word.

    GUIL (_____) RAIN

14. What are the next two letters in this series?

    D S G Q J O M (___) (___)

15. Underline the word that would go in the middle if they were arranged in order.

    castle   kennel   flat   tent   mansion   bungalow   house

16. Underline the two words which must change places.

    Who knows John to find where with the red hat

17. Write down the next letter in the series.

    E I G J I K K (___)

18. Underline the word in brackets which can go with both pairs of words at each end of the bracket.

    breed, rear   (raise, over, pay,)   lift, promote

19. If 8978 means HIGH, what does 214 mean? (_____)

20. Underline the two words, one from each set of brackets, that mean almost the same.

    (king, kingdom, country)   (realm, aristocrat, place)

Unit Four

This test is about how different pairs of pictures go together. Look at these two:

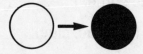

They go together because they are the same shape but there is an important difference. One circle is white and the other is black. In the questions below you will be shown two pictures like the ones above and then you will be shown a third picture. You must find a fourth picture which goes with the third picture which will make a pair in the same way that the first two pictures make a pair.

Look at this example:

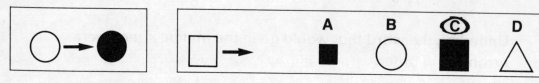

You can think about it, like this. White circle is to black circle as white square is to black square. The correct answer is therefore C which has been circled.

Now try this example:

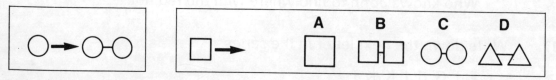

The answer is B. If you got it wrong ask someone to explain. Otherwise begin the test.

Test Four starts here

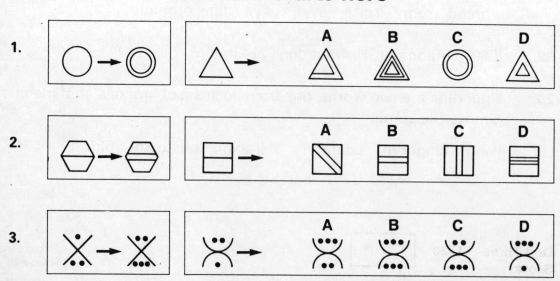

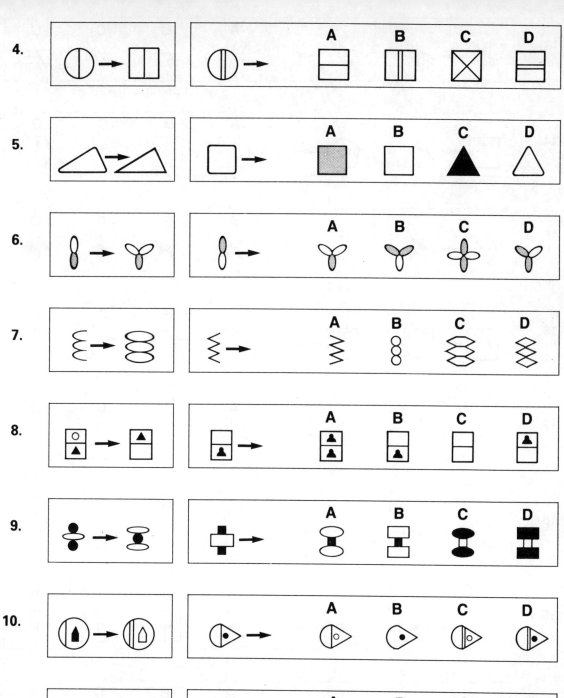

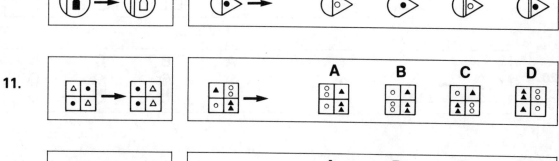

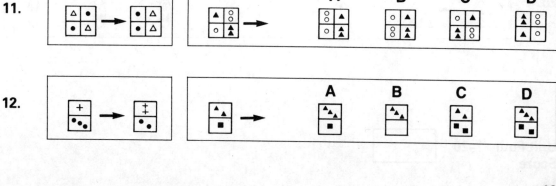

13.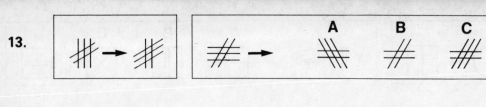

14.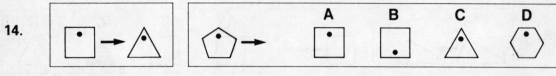

15.

16.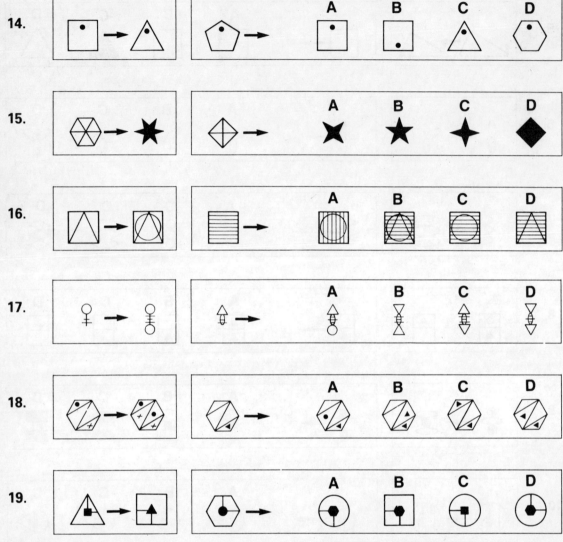

17.

18.

19.

20.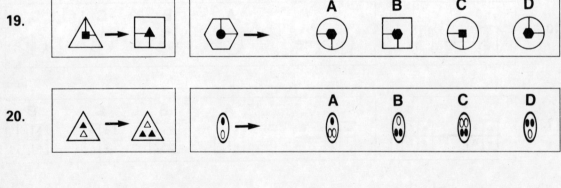

A note to parents

Important: read this before your child starts work.

About the tests
The tests are intended for children to complete with as little adult help as possible. The three areas – verbal, non-verbal and spatial – correspond to the most commonly assessed areas of reasoning. The units within each area allow the child to become familiar with the types of question often used in reasoning tests. The correct answer to each question is given in the answer key. You may wish to mark the child's work yourself, but the child could easily mark and correct some of the sections.

The tests are not designed to enable you to compare the intelligence of the child with that of other children. You should consider the tests as useful reasoning test experience. Their main purpose is to familiarize a child with a range of different reasoning activities. This should help the child to show more fully what he or she can do if a more formal test is taken later on.

Getting the child started
Most children will need some help in starting to use the booklet. Approach the tests as a kind of game or quiz, making sure the questions are tackled seriously, but do not let the child become over-anxious about the results. There is no need to approach the units in any particular order, but spend a little time with the child at the beginning of each one to make sure that he or she has a grasp of what is required. There is no time limit for any of the units but you should encourage reasonably quick working since formal reasoning tests are usually strictly timed.

What to do when the child has finished a Unit
Use the answer key in this centre page pull-out to tick each correct answer. The total number of ticks may then be entered in the score box at the end of the unit.

How to use the Scores Table on page 28
This is designed to bring together the scores for all nine units. You may then find a total score for each of the three areas of reasoning. Be wary of considering relatively low scores in any particular area as a definite sign of weakness. The difficulty of the questions is different from area to area.

What to do about low scores
Children will vary greatly in their scores. While it is tempting to interpret these variations as differences in reasoning ability, it is important to realize that this is not necessarily true. Lack of familiarity with the types of questions or with the method of answering can quite easily result in low scores. Remember that some children require more practice than others before they can show what they can really do. Some children may not do their best because they are over-anxious, whilst others may not have taken the tasks seriously enough. You cannot, therefore, take a low score as meaning that the child definitely has poor reasoning ability.

If, however, the child does not score highly on any or all of the tests do not cause anxiety by expressing disappointment or by chastising. Take the opportunity to discuss wrong answers. This will help you understand how the child reasons, and will also help the child to understand what is required. If the child does not understand your explanations, he or she may not be ready to complete the booklet. Perhaps they are too young or would benefit from other experiences, as suggested on the inside back cover.

Sometimes a child will get a low score in one particular area. Perhaps there is a preference for spatial tasks rather than verbal ones, for example. Such differences as these help to demonstrate that reasoning is a complicated ability to understand. We all show a remarkable diversity of reasoning skills and we all have strengths and weaknesses. The skills tested here cannot hope to cover the whole range. Some children's best strengths will in fact lie outside the scope of this booklet.

Finally, you should remember that some units are generally more difficult than others. Low scores may be reflecting this rather than the child's level of ability. Some of the individual questions are also, purposefully, rather difficult so that all children will find some parts of the booklet a real challenge. Remember that no child is expected to get full marks. If you simply treat each unit as an experience of reasoning tasks from which the child can learn you will be making the most effective use of this booklet.

Further activities

No matter how well the child does, certain activities involving reasoning can be valuable as part of a child's general development. This does not mean that the questions in this booklet should be practised excessively. Simple familiarization with the types of question given here is normally sufficient to enable children to show their best ability when sitting formal tests. To develop the child's reasoning further you could encourage thinking in a variety of ways. Talking, questioning and playing can all help – especially if they involve challenges or novelties. Much of a child's ordinary school work requires reasoning and problem solving and so these kinds of activities should be encouraged. However, other activities for you to enjoy with the child are suggested on the inside back cover.

Remember, children learn better when they are not anxious and when things are enjoyable and fun. They also have a different view of the world which, as adults, we sometimes fail to understand. If they do not reason like we do it is quite normal. They will learn adult methods in due course. Like everything else, mature reasoning develops slowly and we should nurture its development, not force it on at too great a pace.

Answer Key

Unit One

1.	A
2.	B
3.	B
4.	A
5.	B
6.	B
7.	B
8.	C
9.	D
10.	B
11.	B
12.	D
13.	B
14.	A
15.	D
16.	A
17.	D
18.	C
19.	D
20.	C
21.	D
22.	D
23.	C
24.	B
25.	C

Unit Two

1.	B
2.	D
3.	C
4.	B
5.	D
6.	A
7.	D
8.	B
9.	B
10.	A

Unit Three

1.	lake, boy
2.	12
3.	GIRL
4.	sit, stand
5.	P
6.	H
7.	jog
8.	afternoon, eventful
9.	EV
10.	spring
11.	HIT
12.	hint, clue
13.	T or D
14.	M, P
15.	bungalow
16.	John, where
17.	L
18.	raise
19.	BAD
20.	kingdom, realm

Unit Four

1.	D
2.	B
3.	A
4.	B
5.	B
6.	B
7.	D
8.	D
9.	B
10.	C
11.	A
12.	B
13.	C
14.	A
15.	C
16.	C
17.	C
18.	D
19.	A
20.	B

Answer Key

Unit Five

1. C, F
2. A, F
3. C, H
4. B, H
5. E, G
6. E, F
7. E, F
8. B, J
9. C, H
10. B, H

NB. 2 marks for
each question, i.e.
out of 20.

Unit Six

1. A
2. C
3. D
4. A
5. A
6. C
7. B
8. A
9. C
10. B

Unit Seven

Row

1–4. T, F, T, F
5–8. D, T, T, T
9–12. T, F, T, F
13–16. T, T, F, D
17–20. D, D, T, F
21–24. F, F, T, D
25–28. T, F, D, F
29–32. F, T, F, D
33–36. T, D, D, F
37–40. F, T, F, T
41–44. F, F, F, D
45–48. D, F, D, F
49–52. T, F, F, D
53–56. T, D, T, T
57–60. D, D, F, T

Unit Eight

1. B
2. C
3. D
4. A
5. D
6. C
7. D
8. D
9. B
10. D
11. C
12. B
13. A
14. C
15. D

Unit Nine

1. D
2. C
3. A
4. B
5. A
6. B
7. D
8. C
9. B
10. B
11. E
12. D
13. C
14. E
15. C
16. C
17. E
18. A
19. E
20. C
21. A
22. A
23. D
24. D
25. B

Unit Five

Look at these shapes:

Can you see the two question marks? You must decide which are the next two shapes in the series like this:

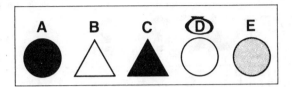 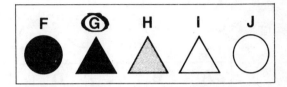

You can see that the series goes black triangle, white circle, black triangle, white circle, black triangle. The next shape must be a white circle. In the 1st box of choices A B C D E we have therefore marked choice D. The next shape after that must be another black triangle and so we have marked choice G in the 2nd box.

Now try this example before you read on.

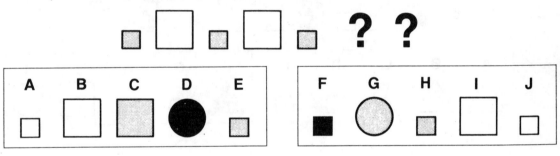

You should have marked choice B in the 1st box and choice H in the 2nd box. If you got them wrong ask someone to explain before beginning the test. Remember whilst doing the test that you will only get circles, triangles and squares but they can be black, white or shaded. They can also be big or small like these:

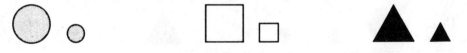

Test Five starts here

1.

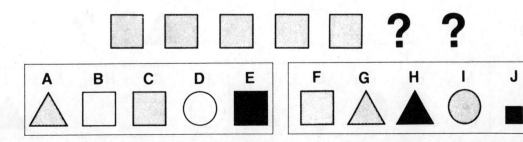

15

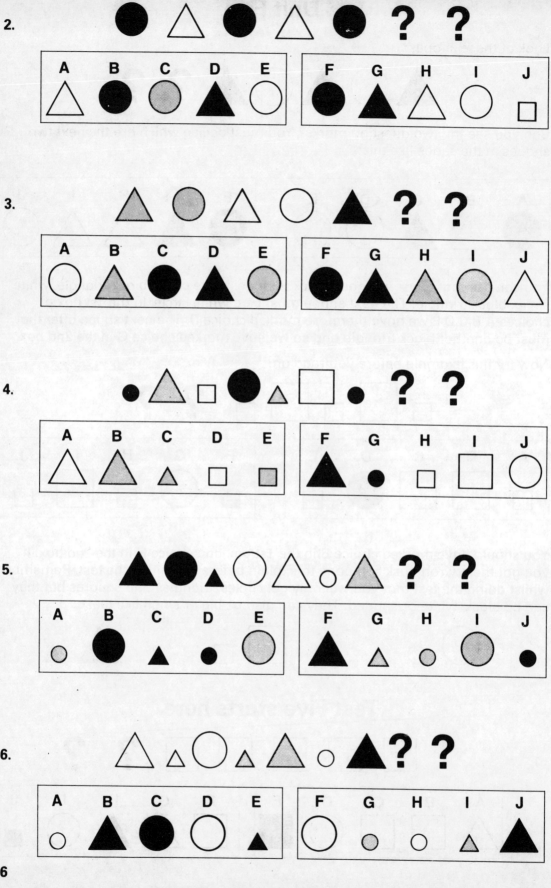

2.

3.

4.

5.

6.

16

7.

A	B	C	D	E		F	G	H	I	J
□	△	■	▲	△		□	△	▲	△	■

8.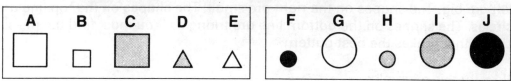

A	B	C	D	E		F	G	H	I	J
□	□	■	△	△		●	○	●	●	●

9.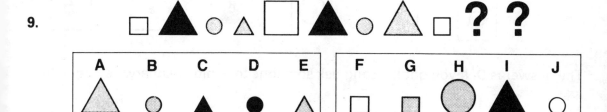

A	B	C	D	E		F	G	H	I	J
△	●	▲	●	△		□	■	●	▲	○

10.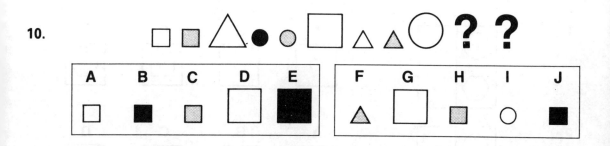

A	B	C	D	E		F	G	H	I	J
□	■	■	□	■		△	□	■	○	■

Unit Five 1–20
Score

Unit Six

Look at these shapes:

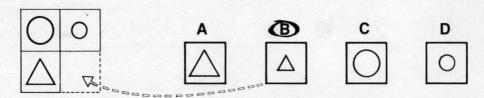

One of the four pieces A, B, C or D is missing from the bottom corner of the large square on the left. Which one is it? The answer is B as shown. The shapes on the left are big. The shapes on the right are small. The shapes on the top line are circles. The shapes on the bottom line are triangles. You must find the missing shape that makes the best pattern.

Now try this example:

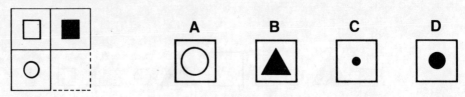

The answer is D. If you got it wrong ask someone to explain. Otherwise begin the test.

Test Six starts here

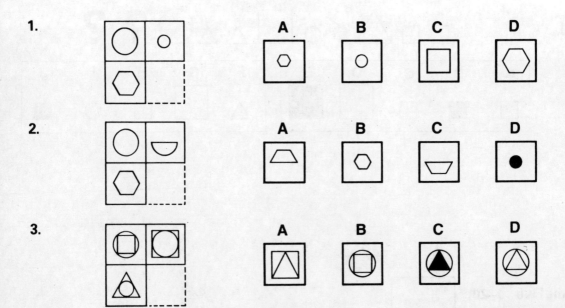

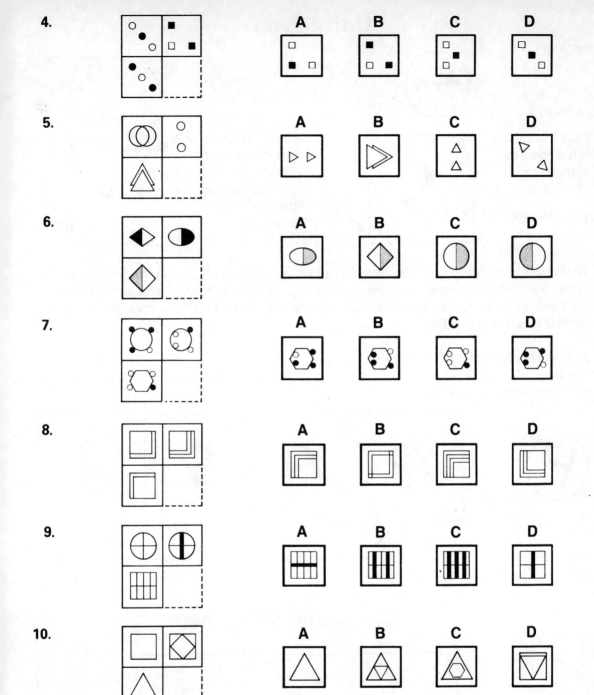

4.

5.

6.

7.

8.

9.

10.

A   B   C   D

Unit Seven

Look at this shape:

Here it is again but it has been turned a bit.

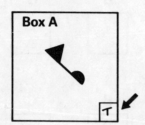

Here it is again but it has been flipped over. It cannot look like this simply by turning it.

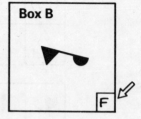

To show that a shape has been turned but not flipped we write T in the box shown in box A by the black arrow. To show that a shape has been flipped over we write F in the box as shown in box B by the white arrow. If a shape has been changed then we write D to show it is different.

In this test you look at the shape in the circle and decide which of the ones to its right has been turned (T), flipped (F) or is simply different (D). Try these examples. The first one has been done for you.

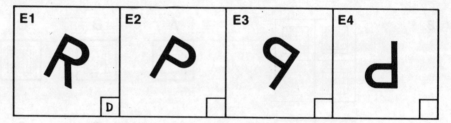

The answers are D, T, F and T in that order. If you cannot see why, ask someone to explain. Otherwise begin the test.

Test Seven starts here

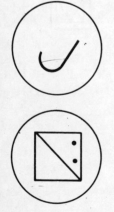
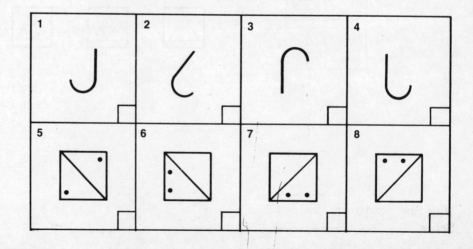

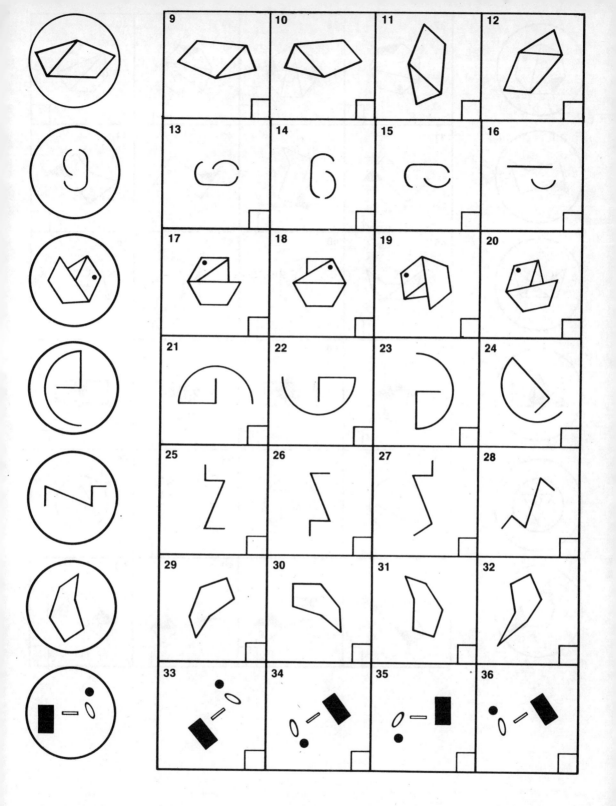

21

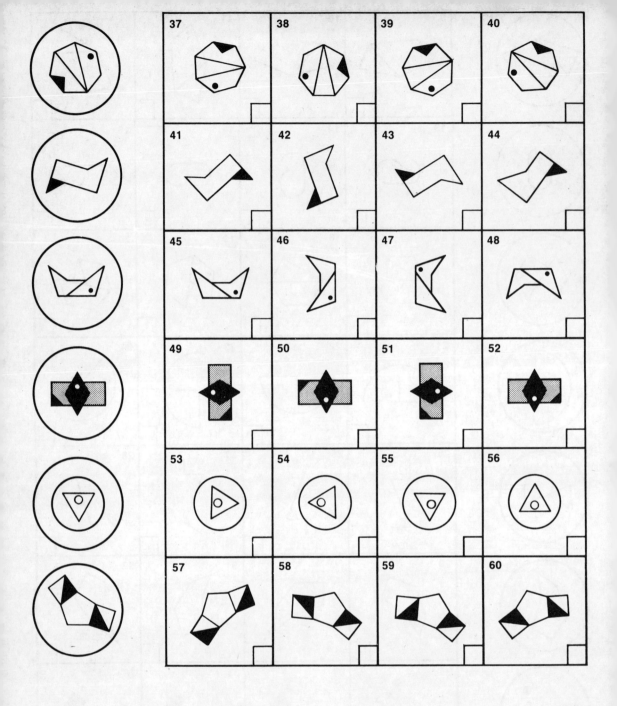

Unit Eight

Look at these shapes:

You can see that the two on the left go together because they are the same shape but one is a bit smaller than the other. Can you see that the other two go together in the same way?

In this test you must see how the two shapes on the left go together and then make a pair on the right so that they go together in the same way:

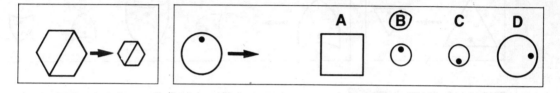

Can you see that choice B makes the best pair on the right that goes together in the same way as the pair on the left. Now try this example before reading on:

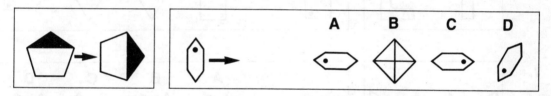

You should have made choice C. If you didn't, ask someone to explain. Then begin the test.

Test Eight starts here

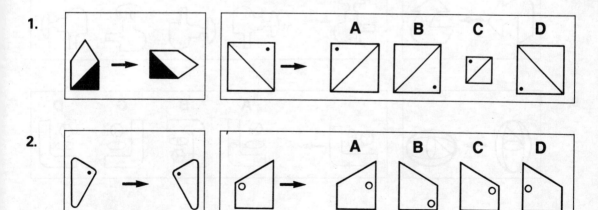

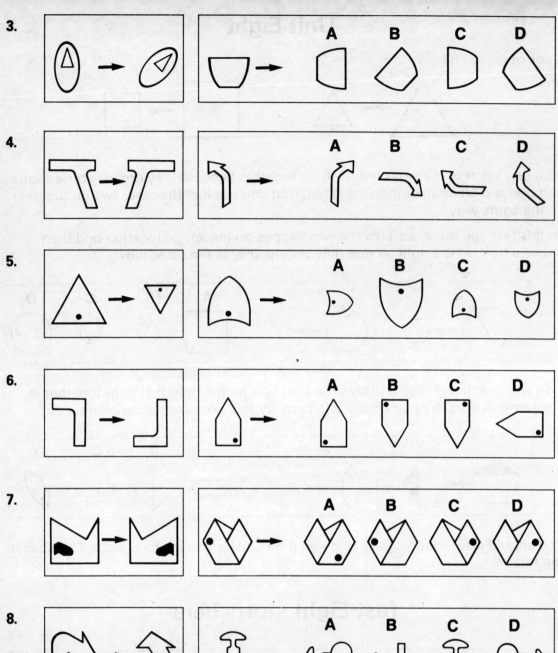

3.

4.

5.

6.

7.

8.

9.

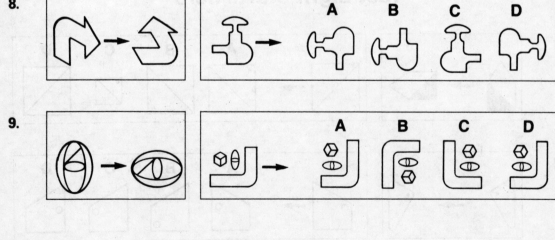

24

10.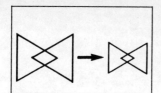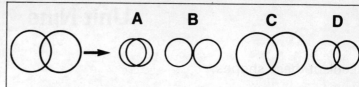

11.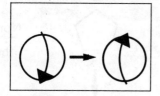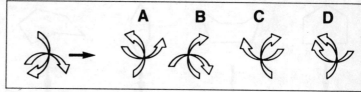

12.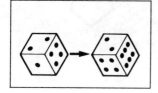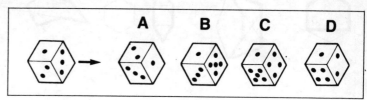

13.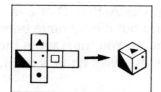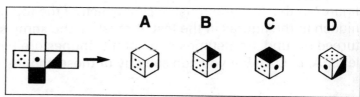

14.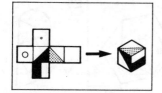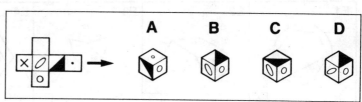

15.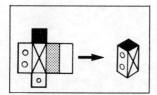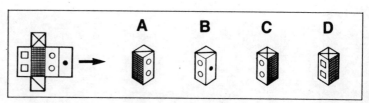

Unit Nine

Look at these shapes:

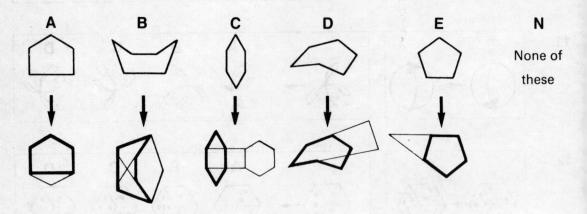

Can you see how each top shape is hidden in the more complicated bottom figure? In this test you must decide which of the top figures A, B, C, D or E is hidden in the figures in the test. It must be the same size but it may have been turned around. Sometimes none of the shapes are hidden. You must write the letter A, B, C, D, E if you can see any of these shapes. Otherwise write N for none.

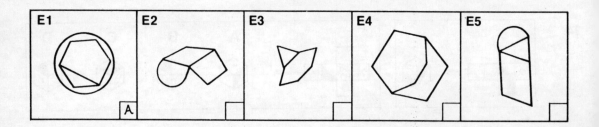

The answers are   E1) A   E2) D   E3) C   E4) B   E5) N

If you got any wrong ask someone to explain. Then begin the test.

Test Nine starts here

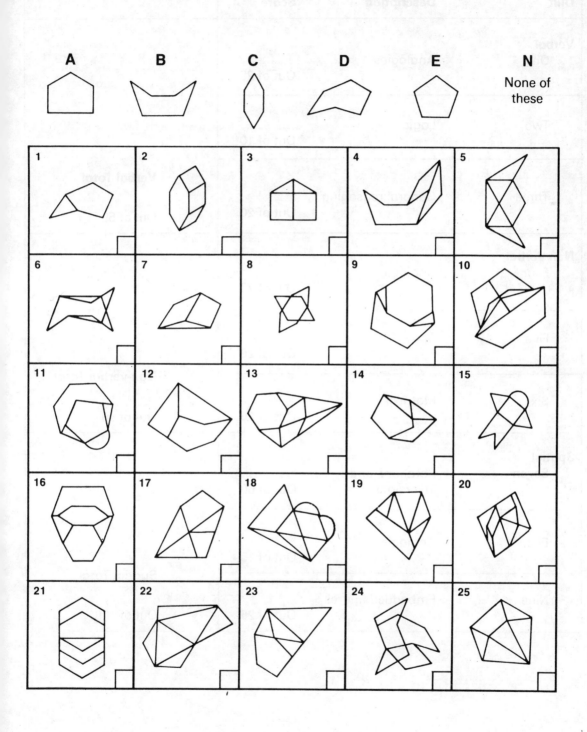

Scores Table

Unit	Description	Score	
Verbal			
One	Analogies	.... Out of 25	
Two	Logic	.... Out of 10	
Three	General reasoning	.... Out of 20	**Verbal Total** .... Out of 55
Non Verbal			
Four	Analogies	.... Out of 20	
Five	Series	.... Out of 20	
Six	Matrices	.... Out of 10	**Non-verbal Total** .... Out of 50
Spatial			
Seven	Rotations and inversions	.... Out of 60	
Eight	Analogies	.... Out of 15	
Nine	Embedded figures	.... Out of 25	**Spatial Total** .... Out of 100